The Rainbow Serpent and Other Stories

James Vance Marshall

T0385988

Level 1

Retold by Paul Shipton
Series Editors: Andy Hopkins and Jocelyn Potter

1.1 What's the book about?

Talk about the animals and birds in these pictures.

1 Do you know their names in your language?
2 They are all from one country. Which country?

lyrebird

butterfly

dingo

cockatoo

owl

rainbow serpent

frog

eaglehawk

caterpillar

platypus

beetle

kangaroo

wombat

1.2 What happens first?

Look at the pictures in the first story. Who or what arrives on the Earth first? And then? What do you think? Write 1–6.

◯ rain

◯ people

◯ mountains

◯ animals

◯ the Rainbow Serpent

◯ trees and flowers

The Rainbow Serpent Brings Animals onto the Earth

The Rainbow Serpent went back to the dark place
under the Earth. 'Come, animals,' she said.

After a long, long sleep in the dark place under the **Earth**, the Rainbow Serpent opened her eyes. She looked at the young Earth. It had no animals, no trees.

'I do not like this place,' the Rainbow Serpent said. She looked up and said, 'Come, rain.'

The rain came down. It rained for days and weeks and months and years. Now there were rivers on the Earth.

The Rainbow Serpent moved across the Earth, and then there were **mountain**s. After that there were trees and **flower**s. But there were no animals.

The Rainbow Serpent went back to the dark place under the Earth.

'Come, animals,' she said.

Earth /ɜːθ/ (n) There are many countries on the *Earth*.
mountain /ˈmaʊntən/ (n) Everest is a big *mountain* in Nepal and Tibet.
flower /ˈflaʊə/ (n) There are beautiful yellow *flowers* in my garden.

First, the **land** animals came out – the kangaroos and the dingoes and the wombats. Some went to the mountains. Some stayed under the trees. Some went to the rivers. They liked this new Earth.

'Come, **bird**s,' the Rainbow Serpent said. And the birds came out. They went up, up, up into the blue.

Then the **fish** and the frogs came out. They went quickly into the water.

Then the **insect**s came out into the new Earth – the beetles and the butterflies. They looked for homes across the new land.

After these animals, a Man and a Woman came onto the Rainbow Serpent's new Earth. The Rainbow Serpent was a good teacher to them. They had food and drink, and they were happy.

'This is not your Earth,' the Rainbow Serpent said to them. 'Be good to it. Be good to the animals here.'

'Yes,' the Man and the Woman answered. 'We understand.'

The Rainbow Serpent was happy with this answer. She started to go back to her dark place under the Earth.

'And now,' she said, 'I am going to sleep.'

land /lænd/ (n) Big animals live here because there is a lot of *land* and not many people.
bird /bɜːd/ (n) In summer the *bird*s sit in a tree near my window.
fish /fɪʃ/ (n) There was a big *fish* in the river.
insect /ˈɪnsekt/ (n) You usually find a lot of *insect*s in hot countries.

The Kangaroo Makes a Friend

'I cannot see very well and I cannot walk very well,' the wombat said. 'I have no friends. But I want water. Can you take me to a river?'

'Stay near me,' Mother Kangaroo said to her son. But little Joey liked to see new things; he liked to meet new animals. He did not want to stay near his mother.

One day, a wombat came to the two kangaroos. He was very old and not very strong.

'I cannot see very well and I cannot walk very well,' the wombat said. 'I have no friends. But I want water. Can you take me to a river?'

Mother Kangaroo looked at the old wombat. 'Come with us,' she said. 'We are going to find water now.'

The old wombat went with the kangaroo and her son. It was very difficult for Mother Kangaroo. Joey moved very quickly, but the wombat walked very slowly. They arrived late at the water.

After a long, long drink, the wombat looked at Mother Kangaroo and said, 'I want food now!'

Mother Kangaroo did not want to say no to a little, old animal. 'Come with us,' she said to him.

The wombat went with the kangaroo and her son again. Again, it was very difficult for Mother Kangaroo. Again, the wombat was very slow, but this time Joey did not want to walk. After a long, long time, they arrived at a good place for food. The old wombat started to eat.

Suddenly, there was a noise. There was a Man near the wombat! The Man started to run.

'The wombat is old and slow,' Mother Kangaroo said to her son. 'The Man is going to catch him.'

She moved quickly across the land. The Man looked at her. Then he started to run after her. The Man was quick, but Mother Kangaroo was very quick. She went up mountains, and then she went down mountains. The Man did not catch her. After a long time, he stopped. He went home with no wombat and no kangaroo.

Mother Kangaroo went back, but her little son Joey and the wombat were not there. Where were they? She looked and looked.

'Joey, where are you?' she said. She was very unhappy. Where was her little son?

She looked under a tree . . . He was there! He opened his eyes and looked up at her with a big smile.

'Where is the old wombat?' Mother Kangaroo asked.

'He went away,' Joey said. 'He was here – and then he wasn't!'

But the old animal was not a wombat. Mother Kangaroo and Joey did not know it, but he was the Great Creator*!

The Great Creator wanted to find a good animal on this Earth, and Mother Kangaroo was very good to the old wombat. Now the Great Creator wanted to be good to the kangaroo.

In the morning, there was a little bag near Mother Kangaroo. This bag was from the Great Creator, but Mother Kangaroo did not understand.

'Where did this come from?' she said. 'And what can I put in it?'

And then, suddenly, the bag was not there. It was *in* her coat of **fur**.

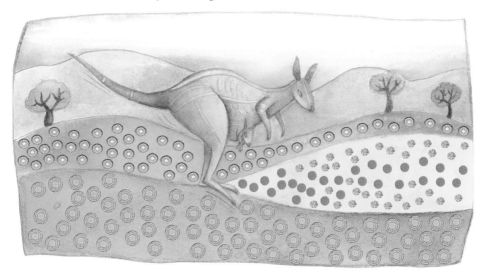

Mother Kangaroo smiled. 'Joey can stay in here. He can sleep and never be cold,' she said. 'And he cannot run away.'

Today, all young kangaroos are 'joeys', and their place is with their mother, in that same bag of fur. Mother kangaroos are happy now – because one kangaroo was a good friend to an old wombat.

---

* The Great Creator: the father, and teacher, of people on Earth in some places in Australia. In some places, it is the Rainbow Serpent.

fur /fɜː/ (n) Animals in cold places usually have a lot of *fur*.

2.1 Were you right?

Look at your answers to Activity 1.2 on page ii. Which arrived first? And then? Number these pictures 1–9.

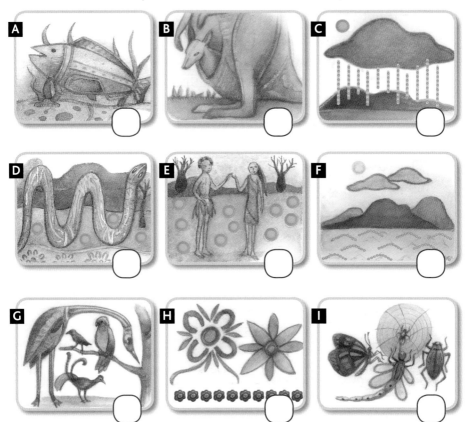

2.2 What more did you learn?

Circle the right answers.

1 The Man and the Woman are happy on Earth.   Yes   No

2 The Rainbow Serpent makes the mountains, flowers,
   land and animals.   Yes   No

3 The kangaroo runs after the Man.   Yes   No

4 The Man catches the wombat.   Yes   No

5 The Great Creator is happy with the kangaroo.   Yes   No

2.3 Language in use

Look at the sentences on the right. Then finish these sentences with verbs from the box. Put the verbs in the past tense.

> The Rainbow Serpent **opened** her eyes.
>
> The Rainbow Serpent **moved** across the Earth.

| arrive | like | look | smile | start |

1 The animals ....liked............ this new Earth.

2 The insects .... for homes across the new land.

3 They .... late at the water.

4 The Man .... to run after her.

5 Joey .... at his mother.

2.4 What happens next?

Look at the pictures on pages 8–11. Write answers to these questions. What do you think?

1 What is the lyrebird going to teach the frog?

....

2 Does the platypus want to be a land animal, a bird or a fish?

....

The Frog Finds a Voice

*The little frog started to sing. His voice was beautiful
and the frogs all listened. But the moon did not move.*

In the early days of the Earth, there was a lyrebird with a beautiful
voice. In the mornings she came to the water and **sang**. The
animals loved to listen to her.

One animal in the water always listened to the lyrebird. He was
a little green frog. He came out of the water and looked at the bird
with his big eyes.

'Hello,' the lyrebird said to him. 'Can you sing?'

The frog only moved his head – no.

'Can you talk?' the lyrebird asked.

The frog moved his head again – no.

Suddenly, there was a voice in the lyrebird's head. It was the voice
of the Great Creator, and it said, 'This little animal is your brother.
You can sing. Teach him.'

'Yes,' the bird answered.

She started to teach the little green frog. She worked with him for
days and days. And, after a lot of work, the frog's voice was good.

The lyrebird was very happy about this. 'Now you can sing,' she
said.

voice /vɔɪs/ (n) He talks in a very quiet *voice*.
sing /sɪŋ/ (v, past: **sang**) (v) We danced and *sang* all night with our friends.

The animals wanted to hear the frog. They came, but then they looked at the little green animal. 'Oh no!' they said. But the frog started to sing and the animals loved his beautiful new voice.

That night, the frog was very happy. 'I can sing!' he said. 'My voice is beautiful!' He said this again and again.

The frog had a little girlfriend. 'Please be quiet now,' she asked. But the little green frog did not stop. 'I can sing! Listen to me! Listen! The **moon** is going to come down to the Earth and listen to me!'

The girl frog smiled. 'I want to see that,' she said. 'Sing to the moon!'

The little frog started to sing. His voice was beautiful and the frogs all listened. But the moon did not move.

On the **next** night the frog tried again. He sang and sang. His voice was very beautiful. But the moon did not come down to the Earth.

On the next night the frog tried again. He sang and sang. But the moon stayed in its place. The frog sang and sang and ...

He stopped. There was a problem with his voice. Only a little **croak** came out of his mouth. He tried again, and he croaked again. His beautiful voice! It was not beautiful now. It was never beautiful again.

Today, frogs come out of the water at night and look up at the moon. But they do not sing. They can only croak.

moon /muːn/ (n) Neil Armstrong was the first man on the *moon*.
next /nekst/ (adj) We went to the cafe again the *next* day.
croak /krəʊk/ (n/v) She is ill and she can only talk in a *croak*.

Man Listens to the Platypus

The platypus listened, but he did not say yes or no.
This was a big question and he wanted to think about it.

I n the early days of the Earth the animals were all friends. But after a time, they were not happy.

The land animals started to talk. 'The animals of the Earth are all good, but we are **special**,' the kangaroo said. 'Look at our fur. Only we have fur.'

But **another** kangaroo said, 'No, look at the platypus. *He* has fur.'

The land animals all went and talked to the platypus. 'Your fur is beautiful,' they said to him. Then they asked, 'Be in our family with us.'

The platypus listened, but he did not say yes or no.

The fish started to talk. One big fish came out of the water. 'The animals of the Earth are all good, but we are special,' she said. 'Only we can swim under the water!'

But another fish said, 'No, the platypus can swim under the water too.'

The fish all went to the platypus. 'You can swim well,' they said to him. 'Be in our family!'

The platypus listened, but he did not say yes or no.

The birds started to talk. One big bird said, 'The animals of the Earth are all good, but we are special! Only we have **egg**s!'

special /ˈspeʃəl/ (adj) She is a *special* friend to me. I love her!
another /əˈnʌðə/ (adj) Do you want *another* drink?
egg /eg/ (n) I like to eat two *eggs* in the morning.

But another bird said, 'No, the platypus has eggs.'

The birds went to the platypus. 'Be in our family,' they asked. 'We have eggs too!'

The platypus listened, but he did not say yes or no. This was a big question and he wanted to think about it.

The animals all waited and waited for the platypus's answer, but it did not come. They all – the birds, the fish and the land animals – went back to his house.

'Be in our family!' the land animals said again.

'No! *Our* family!' the fish said.

'*Our* family!' the birds said.

The platypus listened and he smiled. And then he said, 'I do not want to be in *any* of your families.'

The animals did not like this answer, but the platypus said, 'The Great Creator wanted us on this Earth and we are all special now. We are all special in the eyes of the Great Creator,' he said. 'That is good. We can all live on this Earth and be happy.'

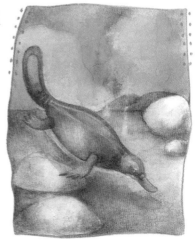

The animals listened to the platypus and smiled. The platypus was right. The animals *were* all special.

A man was there too, behind the animals. He listened to the platypus.

'I am never going to **hurt** the platypus,' he said.

His people said this too. And today they do not hurt this clever little animal.

hurt /hɜːt/ (v) Don't *hurt* your little brother!

11

3.1 Were you right?

Look at your answers to Activity 2.4. Then look at these pictures. What is wrong with them? Correct the sentences.

The frog dances in front of the lyrebird.

....

....

A lot of frogs sing at the moon.

....

....

The platypus wants to be a bird.

....

....

Men hurt platypuses.

....

....

3.2 What more did you learn?

Answer these questions.

1 Why does the lyrebird teach the frog?

Because ....

2 Why does the frog croak?

Because ....

3 What do platypuses *and* birds have?

They ....

4 What do platypuses and kangaroos have?

They ....

3.3 **Language in use**

Look at the sentences on the right.
Then finish these sentences with
words from the box.

> There was a lyrebird **with** a
> beautiful voice.
>
> She came **to** the water and sang.

| about | behind | to | on | out of | under |

1 The frog came .... the water and looked at the bird.

2 'The moon is going to listen .... me!'

3 'The platypus can swim .... the water too.'

4 The platypus wanted to think .... the question.

5 'We can all live .... this Earth and be happy.'

6 The man was there too, ... the animals.

3.4 **What happens next?**

Look at the pictures on pages 14–19. What are you going to read about
now? Tick (✓) the right pictures.

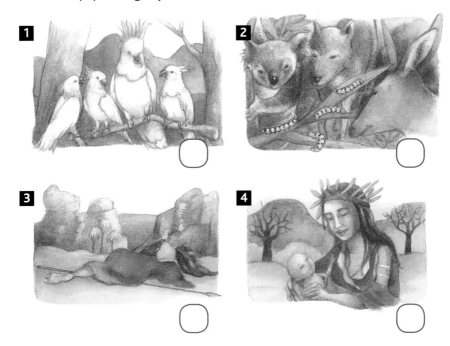

The Caterpillars Answer a Difficult Question

'Talk to us!' the animals said to the bird, but his eyes did not open. The animals opened them, but the bird's eyes did not see. He was dead.

In the early days of the Earth, the animals were all happy. One very old cockatoo liked to sit up in a tree and talk to his friends.

But one day he was not in his tree; he was on his back under the tree. He did not talk and he did not move.

The animals looked down at him.

'Did he fall from the tree?' another bird asked.

'Yes.'

'Talk to us!' the animals said to the bird, but his eyes did not open. The animals opened them, but the bird's eyes did not see. He was dead.

It was the first time on the Earth and the animals did not understand it. 'What is he doing?' they asked. 'And *why*?'

'I know the answer,' said a big eaglehawk. 'Watch this.' With a **stone** in his mouth, he walked to the river. 'The cockatoo is this stone.'

The animals watched. 'What is he doing?' one animal asked.

---

stone /stəʊn/ (n) I can't walk quickly because I've got a little *stone* in my shoe.

'He is putting the stone into the river.'

The stone went down under the water.

'The stone is not here now,' the eaglehawk said, 'and the dead cockatoo is not here now.'

A black bird said, 'That is not right.' With a little **stick** in his mouth, *he* walked to the river.

The animals watched. 'What is he doing?' one animal asked.

'Now he is putting the stick into the water,' another animal answered.

The animals watched the stick. It did not go under the water. It went away down the river.

'The stick is going to another place now,' the black bird said. 'And the dead cockatoo is going to another place too.'

This was difficult for the animals. Which answer was right? They did not know, and they were not happy.

But then some little caterpillars said, 'We know the answer! We know!'

The big animals did not want to listen to these little insects. But then one looked down and said, 'OK, what is your answer?'

'Watch us!' the caterpillars said.

stick /stɪk/ (n) Look! Emma is making a little house with *sticks* in the garden.

The little caterpillars went to sleep for many days and weeks. The winter came and went.

The animals talked about the caterpillars. 'Where are they?' they asked.

But then there was a noise. The animals looked up.

'Look!' one said. 'Butterflies! Butterflies are dancing in the sun!' There were a lot of butterflies and they were very beautiful.

'Look at us!' the butterflies said. 'We were the little caterpillars. But look at us now!'

And then they went to the mountains. The animals watched them.

'How is this an answer to the problem of the dead cockatoo?' one of them asked.

But a clever old owl said, 'I understand. Now the little caterpillars are not here; now they are butterflies. They are special and new, and they are going to a new place in the mountains. Our dead friend is not here now, but he is special and new too. He is in another place.'

The animals were happy with this answer.

A New Flower Comes to the Mountains

She did not want to go back to her friends now. She did not want to move. She did not want to live.

Krubi was a beautiful girl. She lived in the mountains with her people. Many young men loved Krubi, but she loved only one. His name was Bami, and he loved her too.

One day, the men of the mountains were angry.

'This is our land,' Bami said to Krubi. 'But some people are coming into it. They are taking our food.'

'What are you going to do?' Krubi asked.

Bami said, 'We are going to send them away!'

He looked into her big eyes. 'I love you, Krubi,' he said, 'and I am going to come home to you.'

The men went away and Krubi was very unhappy. She walked into the mountains. It was cold up there but Krubi had a red coat with her. She watched Bami and the men of the mountains. They went away from the mountains and across the land.

Krubi stayed and waited. The sun went down, but the men did not come back. Bami did not come back. Krubi waited the next day too. And the next day. But Bami did not come back.

Some of Krubi's friends came to her. 'Don't stay up in the mountains at night,' they said. 'Come back with us.'

But Krubi did not want to go back with her friends. She stayed and waited for Bami.

The moon came up and she waited. The sun came up and she waited.

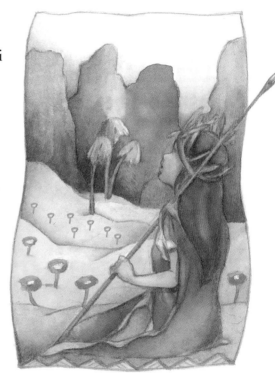

Krubi waited for three long days. Where was Bami?

Suddenly, there was a noise. Krubi looked up. They were back! The men of the mountains were back!

But then Krubi looked again. Bami was not with them.

Krubi's friends came to her again. 'Bami is dead,' they said to her. 'Please come back with us now.'

But Krubi did not go with them. 'Perhaps he is not dead,' she said. 'I am going to stay here and wait for my Bami.'

She waited and waited. But Bami never came back.

'My friends were right,' Krubi said. 'He is dead.'

But she did not want to go back to her friends now. Why go back? She did not want to move; she did not want to live. She closed her eyes, and then she was dead too.

Months came and went. It was very cold, and Krubi's people did not stay in the mountains in those difficult months. But after the winter, the sun came back. Then Krubi's people wanted to come home, home to the mountains.

And now there was a new flower up on the mountain.

It was a beautiful, red **rose**.

'Krubi's coat was this colour,' her old friends said. 'This flower is Krubi. But how?'

'The Great Creator did this,' a clever old man answered. 'Krubi's love for Bami was a beautiful thing. Now we can look at this flower and we can remember her love for him.'

Today you can go and see little red flowers in those mountains. Look at the mountain roses, and remember the story of beautiful Krubi and her love for Bami.

rose /rəʊz/ (n) This beautiful red *rose* is for my girlfriend.

1 **Work with a friend. Ask and answer these questions.**

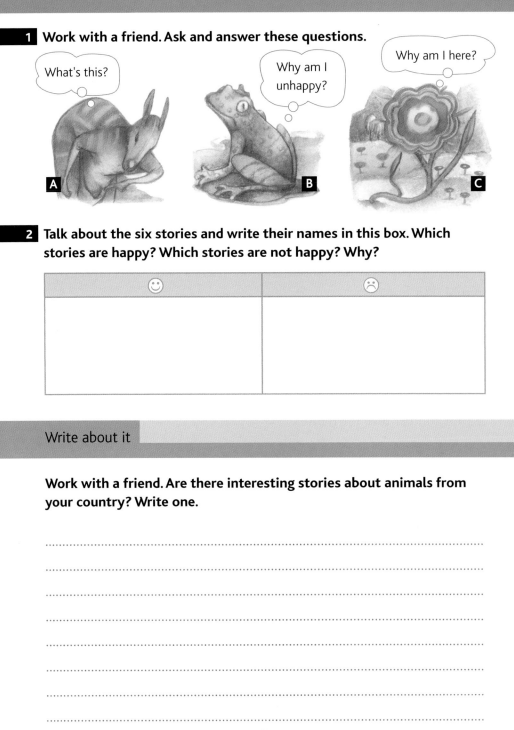

What's this?

Why am I unhappy?

Why am I here?

A

B

C

2 **Talk about the six stories and write their names in this box. Which stories are happy? Which stories are not happy? Why?**

☺	☹

Write about it

Work with a friend. Are there interesting stories about animals from your country? Write one.

....

....

....

....

....

....

....

....

RIGHT OR WRONG?

1 **Talk about these pictures. Who is right? Why? What do you think?**

> I love fur coats.

A

> A family isn't a family with no animals in the house.

B

> I don't eat animals. It's wrong.

C

> The kangaroos are happy here.

D

I DON'T WANT A COCKATOO!

2 **Look at this picture and work with another student. Talk about this problem.**

Student A	You work in this shop. The old woman wants to buy a fish, but you haven't got any fish in your shop. She doesn't know that! Why doesn't she buy a cockatoo? Cockatoos are beautiful birds.

Student B	You are the old woman. You live in a small flat. Listen to the person in the shop. But you don't want a cockatoo – you want a fish!

3 Animals at home

a Do your friends have animals at home? Ask some of them, and write the answers in your notebook. Then talk about your answers.

YES				NO	
Name of student	Which animal(s)?	Why?	Problems?	Name of student	Why not?

b What did people say? Write about their answers.

.... *A lot of /Some /One or two* .... students have animals at home.

They have ....

.... and .... They like having

animals in their homes because ....

....

But .... *all/some/one or two* .... students have problems with their

animals because ....

....

.... *A lot of /Some /One or two* .... students have no animals at

home because ....

....

I .... *have/haven't* .... got any animals because ....

....